YOSEMITE

BILL ROSS

BILL ROSS

ED COOPER

YOSEMITE

Featuring the photography of
Bill Ross
with
Ed Cooper - William Neill - Lewis Kemper

Designed by **Stephen Bennett**
Written by **Peter Jensen**
Edited by **Randy Collings**
Photo editing by **Bill Ross/West Light**

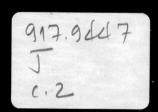
Cover: Half Dome at sunset. Photo by Bill Ross.

Opening spreads in order: sunrise over Half Dome and Tenaya Canyon; photographed from Glacier Point — Rock forms in Tenaya Lake at sunrise — 1612-foot Ribbon Fall, highest of all Yosemite falls — Half Dome at sunset with a last reflection in the Merced River.

Published by
Randy Collings Productions
Box 8658 Holiday Station, Anaheim, California 92892

JAN 5 1982

BILL ROSS

ED COOPER

Yosemite. The Incomparable Valley. The ultimate temple of nature's masterwork. As a shrine accepts its faithful pilgrims, Yosemite National Park today opens her portals to a world in need of nature.

Even today, when reaching the Valley is far less difficult than back in the 1800s (a dusty trip up through the foothills by wagon and horseback), your first view of this vertical world of granite is unforgettable. From the depths of Wawona Tunnel (the Valley's most spectacular approach) you suddenly dive headlong into the light streaming back at you off Half Dome, El Capitan, Cathedral Rocks, The Three Brothers, and the exclamation point of Bridalveil Fall — a brilliant line of white coursing down dark rock walls. The Valley seems so carefully crafted, so balanced in its masses that you might reach out and move granite sentinels like chess pieces on a rumpled board. Even with the sound of automobiles at your back, you stand on the precipice of this first viewpoint and feel the mastery that is impossible to understand with words or images alone.

"So this is Yosemite!" you exclaim in your heart, be it your first trip or your hundredth. This is the valley so indefineable in its grandeur that its most famous chronicler — John Muir —felt helpless in his search for adequate words. Muir spent a lifetime walking Yosemite trails,

John Muir   YOSEMITE NATURAL HISTORY SOCIETY

inching along fissures high above waterfall cauldrons, or locked in debate with defilers who would see Yosemite's wonders exploited or destroyed.

Can a visitor hope to achieve even the smallest fraction of Muir's experience? Or is Yosemite one of nature's unfathomable hieroglyphs that must be studied and visited for a lifetime before being understood?

From your first view of the Valley, Yosemite rewards you. You can camp but a few days amidst trees, hike only a few meadow paths, and only look up at the heavens — and you'll feel the grandeur. Yet you will have missed a lifetime of backcountry travel, the intricacies of Yosemite's natural history, the lexicon of experiences that is only gathered after waking on many a cold morning when the frost crackles on your sleeping bag, or hearing your heart pound wildly as you walk the last of a hundred switchbacks to a throneroom of rock and clouds.

It is in memory of all of your Yosemite experiences — be they of a day or a life — that we offer this book of new images. The Valley changes slowly, and asks much of its photographers. Yet each morning brings a new play of light across the peaks. As no two waves ever break quite the same, so can no day in Yosemite be the same as another.

BILL ROSS

El Capitan's 3000-foot-tall shoulder contrasts with the tracery of decidous trees in icy gowns.

Yosemite. Experience it as you will. It is the shrine of the Sierra.

Yosemite is a geologic battleground: nature locked in a classic dual with herself. No sooner was a land form thrown up than geologic processes began to wear it down. And in Yosemite, there is a feeling of ceaseless weathering even today on the cracked and fissured domes, though it is obvious that Yosemite's supreme struggle took place many thousands of years ago.

The Valley is a gorge about 7 miles long, a mile wide, and a precipitous 3,000 feet deep.

Once the Merced River flowed at a lazy pace over a broad valley. You could have walked from the river to the surrounding hills with scarcely a hitch in your stride, and water eddied in quiet pools long before trout (as we know them) swam the currents. But an uplifting in the earth's crust — as a giant lifts the edge of a table — changed the river's nature. It rushed seaward, and as it went it routed a V-shaped canyon out of ancient granite surfaces. A change of climate brought the ice rivers; glaciers that filled the Merced's canyon and slipped slowly seaward.

LEWIS KEMPER

Beneath the glacier's bulk the granite cracked and sheared. Canyon walls broke off along fissure lines and crumbling rock tumbled like pebbles on a bulldozer blade. Glacial "milk" — water colored white by granite ground as fine as flour — poured from deep inside this icy millstone. Several times the glaciers advanced and receded. When the earth finally warmed again about 9000 years ago, the valley had not only been modified by ice gouging, but the stage was set for the next geologic phase.

BILL ROSS

BILL ROSS

First views of the Valley's magnificence from Inspiration Point as a winter storm moves on. Cars snap on their headlights as they enter Wawona Tunnel: a dark tube blasted through granite.

At sunrise the light moves across the Valley floor in a shadow play and a spotlight of dawn's warmth falls on a lone oak. Flowers raise their heads as the dew departs: red columbine with its eagle claw spurs, and tufts of tall goldenrod.

Photos by BILL ROSS

Half Dome and other spherical-joint surfaces continued to lose their granite layers like skin being pulled off an onion. Ice collected in fractures, expanded, and crowbared the rock apart. Water shaped every streambed, rockfall chute and fissure. Even tiny lichens excreted an acid that ate at the rock. John Muir was living at the base of Sentinel Rock during the Owens Valley earthquake in 1872 and observed rock cascading off the walls.

Yosemite is still in this final phase. Each winter brings change, and in many areas the fresh, unweathered faces of crumbled rock indicate recent rockslides as fissured granite, weakened by expanding ice, lets loose.

Descending into the Valley, you drive roadways ribboning through vanilla-scented Jeffrey pines. Jays swoop about in the trees like acrobats in a leafy Big Top. Once there was an enormous lake backed up here behind a terminal moraine — a huge pile of rock debris left by receding glaciers. Meadows are the remnants of that great lake, and Mirror Lake — the last lake on the Valley floor — is rapidly silting in to complete the "meadowization" of Yosemite Valley.

Twenty-three kinds of lupine thrive in Yosemite. Bridalveil Fall drapes 620 feet then rushes through moss-backed boulders to the Valley floor.
Next pages: El Capitan Meadow blazes with color beneath Middle Cathedral Rock.

ED COOPER

ED COOPER

Host to thousands of visitors a day in the spring, summer and fall, the Valley floor has Yosemite's greatest number of visitor activities. Where to begin? Anywhere but in your automobile.

Valley roads are mostly looping, one-way lanes that can force you several miles out of your way. Free shuttles run to all Valley points in the eastern area throughout the day. They're a marvelous way to see Yosemite without straining to look up from inside your car.

But buses are still buses, and more silent pursuits offer a closeness to the oak woodlands and mixed-conifer forests, and a chance to glimpse a deer or black bear at dusk. Bicycle riding is a popular activity (bikes can be rented at Curry Village and Yosemite Lodge), horses are available, and there are such a variety of ranger-led nature walks that it might take a summer to experience them all.

Inhabitants of the Valley floor aren't limited to bicyclists and campers. Valley forests and meadows are home to the mule deer. In July, reddish-brown fawns follow their mothers on spindly legs.

Less-often seen are the *Ursus americanus* (American black bear). Since the disappearance of the grizzly bear from the Sierra, the black bear has been Yosemite's largest carnivore. They've a gourmet taste for campers' supplies, and though the Park Service keeps an eye on animals that become regular troublemakers, you'll still hear of an occasional car being broken into when visitors leave picnic foods in sight (and in smelling range).

Also prowling the forest paths are mountain coyote, squirrels, chipmunks, "montain meadow" mice, porcupine, skunks, and that whistler of rock piles: the pika — a small, rabbit-like mammal that collects and stores hay in rocky dens, and warns of intruders with a shrill cry.

Overhead are the jesters of the breezes: cocky jays that screech and squawk in the treetops and sneak down into camp to steal a cracker crumb or two.

"Best Dancer" award goes to the water ousel, who can be seen streamside perched on rocks bobbing its body up and down. Ousels sometimes walk upstream *underwater* in search of drifting food. Muir observed: "He is not web fotted, yet he dives fearlessly into foaming rapids, seeming to take greater delight the more boisterous the stream..."

Other Valley and high country birds include the canyon wren, Oregon junco, red-shafted flicker, golden eagle, woodpecker, blackbirds, grosbeaks and hummingbirds.

Rattlesnakes inhabit the west slope of the Yosemite region, but few walkers encounter one of these reclusive reptiles. If you do, simply keep your distance... they're more afraid of you than their fearsome rattle lets on.

The national park's 150 lakes and almost 500 miles of streams could keep a fisherman happy for a lifetime. Rainbow trout cruise the rougher waters in most areas of the park, waiting to rise to a fly or snap at a spinner. Brown trout like quieter holes, and Eastern brook trout will take a hook mostly at high altitudes in frigid waters.

Camping in the Valley is a close-in experience that ranges from tent camping on the north side with other backpackers, to the rustic luxury of tent cabins at Curry Village. Campgrounds are usually full during the summer months and the river sprinkled with bathers floating on air mattresses or watching trout through facemasks. There's a lazy peacefulness to valley campgrounds: many campers use them as a homebase for their daily hikes and activities.

At the heart of it all is Valley Visitor Center, a building that rambles like a bent pinebranch to accommodate exhibits of natural history, geology and park lore. Rangers can answer your questions and arm you with a handful of literature to plan your stay.

In summer especially, the Valley's several fine restaurants pulse with activity, and after dinner (at Yosemite Lodge) there's often a ranger-led campfire program, movie or slide show. If you don't want to camp, the Valley's hotel accommodations range from the modern Yosemite Lodge to the classic Ahwahnee. In the Ahwahnee, a great granite and timber edifice, there's a dining room so large you may walk half the length of a football field to your table.

In springtime, Yosemite's mountains rise again from snow beds and water courses down their flanks. Majestic falls — Yosemite, Bridalveil, Sentinel, Ribbon, Cascade, Vernal, Nevada, Illilouette and others — spout from the cliffs. It is a time for walking, and a Yosemite favorite is the Nevada Fall/Vernal Fall trail.

ED COOPER

Sceptor in a throneroom *of granite: Sentinel Rock. Benchmark on nearby Sentinel Dome was set in lichen-crusted granite.*

Fall is a quieter time in the Valley. Equestrian rangers are ready with friendly advice for late-season visitors, and a campfire takes the cool edge off the night air.

BILL ROSS

BILL ROSS

BILL ROSS

Leaping rainbow plants its feet in the mist of Vernal Fall. In spring, the Mist Trail to the top is a drenching route over slippery, jagged talus. Bring your poncho!

BILL ROSS

BILL ROSS

ED COOPER

23

Seasons pass and the Valley moves from the promise of spring to the heat and buzzing crickets of summer. Then fall paints the trees, until winter slows and silences the woodlands. There is no best time to visit Yosemite: each season is a discovery.

BILL ROSS

BILL ROSS

WILLIAM NEILL

WILLIAM NEILL

WILLIAM NEILL

25

Plan to set off early one morning on the trail from Happy Isles up the canyon to Little Yosemite Valley. Immediately the path grows steep and the roar of the Merced River falls below you as steps take you high up a forested granite wall. First glimpse of Vernal Fall is from the bridge about half a mile below the cataract, and hikers who aren't prepared for a wet, slippery climb should stop here. One prophetic trail sign reads: "You have taken the first step to wilderness. The next step is through the mist to the top of the fall. But wilderness does not lie that close. Steps to wilderness increase as more people reach out for solitude. Continue . . . if you are prepared."

Vernal is a wide curtain of water that courses straight down to a rock ledge, then bounds outward in a cloud of spray haloed with rainbows. As you climb Mist Trail, it steepens into a stairway of carefully set granite blocks. The mist drenches your bent shoulders like rain, glasses fog and cameras need underwater housings to avoid ruin. The last 100 meters to the top is along a cliff face and you cling to the handrail like a nonswimmer holding the edge in the deep end of a pool.

Even at the top of Vernal, with visitors standing close beside you, wilderness draws close. This is Yosemite's water at its most powerful — wrapping over the cliff edge with blue steel tension, then bursting into midair pennants of waving spray.

Behind Vernal Fall is wide Emerald Pool cupped in smooth granite, where hikers often stretch out on the rock "beaches" to sun away the afternoon. Above the pool, the river loses itself on an acre of polished, steep ledges, and your boots would feel like ice skates if you ventured near the water's edge. Signs warn you of getting close to swift water: glaciated granite is extremely slick when wet.

Lashing out *of its granite chute, Nevada Fall is the acrobat of Little Yosemite Valley south of Half Dome.*
Next pages: *Merced River mirrors oaks beneath El Capitan.*

ED COOPER

Photos by BILL ROSS

What is the Yosemite experience? *Much of it is people interacting with each other and nature. Rangers lead popular nature walks. Bicycling on the flat Valley floor is an unmatched way to quietly cover miles of beauty with the wind in your hair and the sweet pine smell of the forests leading you on.*

A brisk morning dip in the chilly waters of the Merced River or an afternoon hike through verdant, fern-laden grottos enhance one's personal experience in the Yosemite, awakening the senses to the wonders of Mother Nature.

BILL ROSS

ED COOPER

BILL ROSS

Darkness fashions trees and rocks into shadow curtains.
Rock-buttressed Ahwahnee Hotel offers elegant
accommodation with a hall-of-the-mountain-king
atmosphere. The hotel was raised by an army of craftsmen
working under the Work Projects Administration. Morning
sun through the trees casts shadows on the California
Chapel in the Valley.

LEWIS KEMPER

Of Yosemite Falls, John Muir wrote: "This noble fall has far the richest, as well as the most powerful, voice of all the falls of the Valley," Like many of Yosemite's cataracts, Yosemite Falls slows to but a trickle in late summer.

The Ahwahnee spreads its sprawling roofs amidst acres of lawns, patios and meadows.

BILL ROSS

CRAIG AURNESS

From Gold to Master Plan: The Valley's Past

It was color in Sierra rivers that brought the first non-Indian visitors to Yosemite. Indians had known of the valley for centuries; it lay on trade routes across the Sierra and the valley floor in warm months was an ideal upland habitat. But it took gold fever to push new visitors closer to the west rim.

The Yosemite, or Grizzly Bear, tribe — alarmed at this sudden invasion of their once serene woodlands — attacked a few miners. It was a terrible, but pridefully unavoidable, mistake. Soon a punitive expedition, the Mariposa Battalion under Major Savage, entered the valley in 1851. Confronting Tenaya, chief of the Yosemites, Savage began efforts to remove the tribe to the Fresno reservation. A 'few years later, Tenaya and his band returned to the valley, but were wiped out by Mono Indians.

In 1855, James Hutchings brought in Yosemite's first sightseers. Soon afterward hotels were opened, roads built, and by 1864 the Valley and Mariposa Grove were granted to the State of California in a historic proclamation by President Lincoln.

John Muir first visited Yosemite in 1868, beginning his lifetime association with the park. In 1890 Muir's articles on Yosemite were published in Century Magazine, and October 1 of that year Yosemite National Park was established.

On an official visit to the newly acquisitioned National Park President Theodore Roosevelt, avid outdoorsman and conservationist, joined John Muir at breathtaking Glacier Point. Overwhelmed by the grandeur of the Sierra, he expressed his awe by describing Yosemite as "the most beautiful place on earth."

By 1913 over a hundred cars a year were making the tortuous trip via Coulterville Road, and by 1915 the park had over 33,000 visitors.

Today Yosemite enters the final decades of the century with a renewed commitment to preservation. A General Management Plan of 1980 recommends eventual elimination of private vehicles from Yosemite Valley and reduction or removal of employee housing, administrative, and maintenance buildings to El Portal. Even if visitor numbers increase, Yosemite will become a quieter, more satisfying place to experience the limitless pleasures of the High Sierra.

Through the notch springs Upper Yosemite Fall. At Ansel Adams Gallery in Yosemite Village you can view (or purchase) photographs by the park's most famous photographer. Teddy Roosevelt stands atop Glacier Point looking over the magnificent valley.

BILL ROSS

37

Photos by BILL ROSS

Great scales *of rock fell away to create Royal Arches beneath North Dome and close beside Washington Column. From Glacier Point, you look down on North Dome, Basket Dome and Indian Ridge.*

Equipped with drinking water and lunch, you can continue on to Nevada Fall's brilliant white mane. Viewed from below, you can see water strike the cliff as turbulently as champagne poured straight into a glass, and white spume lather across the cliff. Even in late summer, when the river is but a fraction of itself, the rumbling, rock-gnashing sound of Nevada and Vernal Falls echoes across the canyon to listeners high atop Glacier Point.

Such is a day hike out of the Valley, one of dozens you can venture on from spring to late fall. Common-sense precautions are important, for every now and then you will see Yosemite's rescue helicopter droning over the cliffs in search of an injured hiker or climber. Stay on the trails and step cautiously, and the only memory you'll have of a day's walk will be your tingling legs, sunburned arms and exhilaration.

Another sidetrip is the drive (or hike on Four Mile Trail) to Glacier Point. If you're an early riser, you'll see hangliders from late spring to early fall swooping off into the misty blue void, silhouetted against Half Dome like manta rays riding the currents. Takeoff time is 8 A.M. (rangers at the Visitors Center can tell you when flights will be allowed). After an experienced pilot-ranger checks out fliers and their gear, pilots run down a stretch of rock for one heartstopping moment. Then they are free, hanging beneath the rustling nylon wings 2,500 feet above the Valley, their shouts of joy echoing off Half Dome. Landing is nearby (but far below) in a broad meadow at the base of El Capitan. Though the flights look perilous, careful supervision has helped prevent serious injury.

One sight from Glacier Point (one that few visitors experience) is the view of the Valley at sunset. Carry a flashlight and stay to watch darkness draw across the meadows. You look straight down from your railing perch as lights blink on in the campsites and lodging areas below, forming a galaxy amidst the dark patches of forest. Above, the Milky Way bands the sky from north to south, and the moon rises slowly behind Half Dome. That's the magic of Yosemite.

BILL ROSS

ED COOPER

In any light, in any season, Half Dome shows her moods. Free double-decker trams loop Valley roads from Happy Isles to Mirror Lake to Yosemite Lodge.

ED COO

Etching a night sky, stars and planets in spectral variety seem to race on circular tracks in this 2½-hour time exposure taken from Glacier Point. A small controlled-burn forest fire glows high on the north rim like a last ember in a black velvet fireplace. Two planes and one meteor cut straight paths above mysterious lights on Half Dome — the flashlights of late-night hikers.

8 A.M. Glacier Point: Ranger does a last safety check and harness hookup for a hanglider pilot. A short sprint down the rock and this fragile birdman will be 3000 feet above Valley meadows.

Next Pages - *"Awoo! It's bee-yoo-tiful!"* yodeled this expert pilot to the watching cliffs. Positioning hands right after takeoff, he readies for a left turn on the long swoop down to El Capitan Meadow.

Photos by BILL ROSS

Photos by ED COOPER

Previous pages: El Capitan and Cathedral Rocks.

A city of rock walls. Yosemite's Three Brothers and El Capitan are doubled in the still-as-a-mirror Merced River. The rocks are a climber's greatest challenge, either on a dihedral wall of El Capitan or swinging like an aerial tram between Lost Arrow Spire and a main wall.

Following pages: El Capitan just after a snowstorm.

ED COOPER

Of the forests of Yosemite, the giant sequoias are its ancient botanical landmarks, some living almost 4,000 years. Three groves preserve them — the Mariposa, Tuolumne and Merced — and they continue to reign as the monarchs of all Sierra forests.

And like some monarchs, the giant sequoias at first struggled for recognition. In 1833, Joseph Walker led a party along the flanks of the High Sierra and apparently stumbled upon "some trees of the redwood species incredibly large — some of which would measure from 16 to 18 fathoms (96 to 108 feet) round the trunk at the height of a large man's head from the ground." Yet all but two of the published journals of the trip perished in a fire, and the trees remained essentially unknown until the "discovery date" of 1852.

It was A.T. Dowd, an employee at the Union Water Company in Murphys, who came across the trees on a backcountry amble. Soon the discovery was trumpeted around the world. But over the years it was another name — Galen Clark — that came to be married to the giant sequoia.

In Mariposa Grove, *new growth struggles upward for light amidst sequoia elders 20 feet in diameter. Mariposa lilies open cream-white petals beside fallen cones.*

In 1857 Clark named Mariposa Grove after the county Mariposa when he set up a stage station at Wawona. Until the age of 96 he was the "Guardian of Yosemite;" leading trips into the valley, writing of its treasures, protecting its resources under state — then federal — ownership, and studying its natural history. Muir called Clark "the best mountaineer I ever met... His kindness to all Yosemite visitors and mountaineers was marvelously constant and uniform." Today Clark is remembered with the Galen Clark Tree, probably the first giant he saw upon entering Mariposa Grove.

A walk through Mariposa Grove is a walk in Yosemite's finest cathedral. The Grove is located near the south entrance to the national park off Highway 41. During the summer months you can ride a tram amidst the dusky trunks and marvel at the size of trees that somehow seem stocky and tremendously tall at the same time. Giant sequoias reach their greatest height in the first 900 years of growth. Then begins a gradual thickening of girth until they reach the proportions of such stout elders as the Grizzly Giant. Some are scarred by lightning from trying to stretch too high above the grove.

In winter, the sequoias' crowns become clouds of snow above a white-mantled forest floor. Snow drifts into the fissured bark, giving the trees the look of a giant's beard flecked with gray. Whenever you visit the groves, you'll leave humbled by the largest living things on earth.

Elsewhere in Yosemite, trees extend their habitats from the valley floor almost up onto the cliffs themselves. Some, like the Jeffrey Pine at Sentinel Point (which died in 1980 from the effects of natural drought), twist their roots deep into crevasses in the most improbable places, their branch forms taking on a bonzai look.

Muir was fond of climbing trees throughout Yosemite. "Climbing these grand trees (yellow pine), especially when they are waving and singing in worship in wind-storms, is a glorious experience. Ascending from the lowest branch to the topmost is like stepping up stairs through a blaze of white light, every needle thrilling and shining as if with religious ecstasy.

Mountain embroidery: pine cones in a bed of lupine.

Fire-scarred and its top shattered by lightning, Grizzly Giant is still the world's largest living thing.

Unawed by its massive neighborhood, raccoon "bandit" makes a rare daytime appearance.

ED COOPER

BILL ROSS

WILLIAM NEILL

Look up *and the giant sequoias converge in the heavens like spears on a target. Many Sierra forests are quite open, unlike the humid forests of the northwest or south. Naked seeds of the conifers or Gymnosperms are borne in cones of many colors and patterns.*

Largest Sierra carnivore*, the black bear ambles through forest and campground, weighs almost 300 pounds.*

CRAIG AURNESS

YOSEMITE PARK & CURRY CO.

BILL ROSS

Photos by BILL ROSS

Raking moisture from advancing storm-fronts, the Sierra sleeps under as much as 50 or 60 feet of snow in some areas. Be it ice crystals caught in pine needles or deep drifts just right for sledding, winter precipitation melts in springtime to feed Yosemite's spectacular falls and rivers.

Tucked in the park's southwest hip pocket, the Wawona area welcomes visitors with a stately hotel (established in 1856 near the Big Trees). At Pioneer History Center you can clatter along in an Express wagon or hear stories of early Yosemite told by young actors in period dress.

Following pages: partial lunar eclipse over Sentinel Dome.

Photos by BILL ROSS

The Tuolumne River loses itself in Tuolumne Meadows, meandering through grassy hillocks before gathering again to plunge down its Grand Canyon. Bluebirds and shooting star flowers thrive in very wet meadows.

Nature's golf course, *Tuolumne Meadows, stretches through a gentle valley skirted by Tioga Road, Rock "bergs" poke up through the deep turf that nurtures paintbrush and delicate leopard lilies. Bluebirds at home in the pine trees.*

ED COOPER

BILL ROSS

BILL ROSS

Balding Lambert Dome dives into Tenaya Lake. Glaciated granite is at its best in this region, planed to a fine polish. A gold skiff of pine pollen spinkles the lake and foreground rocks in late June.

There's a lofty world in Yosemite not of automobiles and campsite reservations, roofs, hot water and the smell of charcoal lighter fluid. Call it the High Country, Yosemite Wilderness, or what you will, it is a place far apart from the comparative hustle and bustle of the valley area, a place where you're likely to have a half day to yourself with just an errant cloud, silvery peak and chuckling stream as your companions.

Only one road crosses the park: the legendary Tioga Road. Until 1961 it remained a gravelly challenge with thousands of curves — and boulders at road's edge that hungered for a bite of a fender. Its 60 miles originally were laid out to haul supplies to a mine (and hopefully equal wagonloads of wealth out), but with the automobile more sightseers than ore began venturing over the uneven surface, and eventually it was paved through to Lee Vining on the east side of the Sierra.

Because the high heartland is touched only by Tioga Road, Yosemite National Park's 1189 square miles remain mostly wilderness. Only visitors on foot or horseback can come close to the Grand Canyon of the Tuolumne, Mount Lyell, Cathedral Range, and the myriad spurs and valleys of the Sierra's main crest.

Photos by BILL ROSS

Some haughty California gulls make their summer home at Tenaya Lake. Sailors and fishermen also ply the sweet snow-melt water. On Tioga Pass, Yosemite's east entrance, you car (and you) gasp for air in the altitude and breathtaking view of a shallow tarn with Mammoth Peak in the distance.

Hikers usually start from the Valley floor on the Tenaya Lake and Tuolumne Meadows Trail, the John Muir Trail, or the Yosemite Creek Trail up past Yosemite Falls. Or you can drive deep into the park on Tioga Road and head north or south from Tuolumne Meadows.

Whenever you begin, check in (if you'll be out overnight) for permits with the National Park Service at any permit-issuing station (the main station is Valley Visitor Center).

Yosemite's backcountry greets the prepared hiker kindly: there are a tremendous number of trails. Yosemite Park and Curry Co. maintains five High Sierra camps where you can sleep in dormitory style tents scattered about a central dining tent. Naturally these are popular stopovers and reservations are needed as surely as a good pair of shoes to get you there.

The question of "how much visitor travel is too much?" is constantly examined in Yosemite, for on popular high-country trails you'll pass many a fellow hiker. The trails can grow to deep, eroding ruts, and campsites are increasingly denuded of vegetation. But thoughtful travelers go lightly on the land, burning no wood, packing out all that's packed in, and leaving only footprints.

Best guide to the high country is "Sierra Nevada Natural History" (Tracy Storer and Robert Usinger, University of California Press). From owls to owl clover, pines to pondweed, caddis fly to crayfish, this guide has every explanation and illustration tucked within its pocket-size covers.

Taillights streak past White Wolf Lodge, still a fine place for a homemade meal and snug bed. In the high country, sturdy-legged backpackers negotiate jumbled-rock trails, or families camp closer to roadheads — like here at White Wolf, a good jumping-off point for day hikes.

CHUCK O'REAR

BILL ROSS

BILL ROSS

BILL ROSS

With your saddlebags or pack full, you can explore the park's "99 percent" — the backcountry that only 1 percent of Yosemite visitors see. High Sierra camps like Glen Aulin (reached by this bridge over the Tuolumne) are spread at one-day-hike intervals through the park.

Glacial polish is the ice age's footprint — seen throughout the Grand Canyon of the Tuolumne on its roller coaster dive to Hetch Hetchy.

Hiking the high country is a celebration of natural history; even the clouds of mosquitoes that surround your head and hands on a still evening in spring are a reminder that a great cycle is unfolding. The mosquito that feasts on your hand one night may be food for a flashing trout the next.

Above it all, the Sierra Crest is a proscenium arch to the weather drama, standing high to the east of the great Central Valley and coastal staging areas for storms. Coast ranges snag some of the rain marching in off the Pacific, but a great mass of moist air flows in from the Golden Gate to the Sierra unimpeded, and so it is that the central Sierra gets the most snow. Yosemite is a bit south, but deep drifts and summer storms are still common.

In a summer squall, the clouds build in white haystack heaps darkening to black at the base. Summits seem to saw at the base of each cumulus until lightning cracks into the afternoon gloom and the first lancers of rain brush across granite faces.

A day on the trail can be spent in one diversion after another. A 40-year-old feels like a toddler discovering a new neighborhood. Try to put aside thoughts of covering ground and yield to examining the bright spike of a snow plant pushing through the moldering forest duff, or watch the furry head of a marmot as it checks your approach.

You could spend days walking slowly over the glacial highways: tracing the ice scars on hump-backed granite domes and feeling rock worn smooth as window glass. Trails are sprinkled with laboring hikers who exclaim of their mileage as you pass on a switchback: "Whew! 18 miles today. We've come all the way from Vogelsang."

Find what challenge you will in the High Country. For some hikers it's distance, for others, solitude. And others, study. They all seek revitalization. Muir once described city dwellers as "All are more or less sick; there is not a perfectly sane man in a city . . ." Harsh words, but meant more as a reminder that there is no solace in canyons of buildings. "Nevermore, however weary, should one faint by the way who gains the blessings of one mountain day; whatever his fate, long life, short life, stormy or calm, he is rich forever."

BILL ROSS

Last to catch the alpenglow, high clouds show off at day's end. Muir called the Sierra the "Range of Light," and every evening reaffirms his early observation.

Following pages: icy Tioga Lake unlocking in a spring thaw with Mt. Dana behind. Coyotes prowl the drifts, still surprised to see man in winter.

THE END
Randy Collings Productions

Published for and in behalf of
Yosemite Park & Curry Co.